INTRODUCTION

This book is filled with ideas for catechists, teachers, and families who walk with children on their faith journey. Pope Francis said, "I invite all Christians, everywhere, at this very moment to a renewed personal encounter with Jesus Christ" (*Joy of the Gospel*).

We want children to know that Jesus Christ is already here present in their lives, and that he loves them without end. Then they will be able to respond to the love of Jesus. The learning experiences in this book will help them explore ways they can encounter Jesus Christ in their heart, in other people, in prayer, in the gospels, in serving others, by living as peacemakers, and by sharing the good news.

The learning experiences in this book will help guide children as they learn about having a relationship with Jesus and with other people. Each idea is divided into three parts—message, activity, and prayer. The children learn what Jesus Christ shows us by his words and actions in the gospels.

It is important for children to understand that Jesus calls each of us to be his disciples. We want children to say yes to walking with Jesus and

TWENTY-THIRD PUBLICATIONS, A division of Bayard, Inc.
One Montauk Avenue, Suite 200 • New London, CT 06320
(860) 437-3012 or (800) 321-0411 • www.twentythirdpublications.com

ISBN: 978-1-62785-520-4 • Cover image: Shutterstock.com / Sergey Novikov

Printed in the U.S.A.

being his disciples. We explore how to live in hope each day. The ideas are great for children ages 5–8 but also work well with older children.

This resource can be used in a variety of ways including:

- children's faith formation programs,
- Catholic schools,
- homeschool programs,
- whole community catechesis,
- groups of families,
- individual families of all ages.

The ideas in this book invite children to learn by doing as they walk with Jesus. The variety of things to do will appeal to many different types of children, who learn in different ways. Activities include echo pantomimes, crafts, gospel charades, prayer activities, scenarios, group projects, service ideas, and many others.

These learning activities will help you engage the interest of children as they explore their relationship with Jesus Christ and with one another. With the help of caring people in their lives, children learn to live in joy as disciples.

CHAPTER 1

Encounter Jesus in our hearts

It is so important that we help children encounter Jesus, who is already here in our lives and in our hearts. We are called to have a relationship with him, who loves us without end. We are to follow his way of love each day. We are never alone because Jesus is always with us.

It sometimes seems like we search in all directions for meaning and purpose in our lives. But we sometimes forget that Jesus is already here with us. We just have to open our hearts to see that Jesus was with us all along. We have a purpose. There is a plan for each of our lives. Jesus will show us the way.

It is so important for us to share the love of Jesus Christ with the children in our programs, our schools, our families, and our communities. Only when children know they are loved by our Lord Jesus Christ are they able to respond to that love in their hearts and in their lives. We help children hear the call of Jesus in their hearts and live in joy as his disciples.

Jesus loves each of us

EXPLORE THE MESSAGE

Jesus loves each of us now and always. We do not have to look for Jesus because he is always here with us. Jesus will never stop loving us, no matter what. Jesus shows us God's love for all people.

Jesus said to his followers, "As the Father has loved me, so I have loved you."

» JOHN 15:9

Jesus reminds us that God, who is Father, Son, and Holy Spirit, will guide our lives. Stress to the children that God has loved us since before we were born and will always love us. We don't have to earn that love. God created each of us and thinks we are wonderful and amazing!

Remember that each of us is special to Jesus. We belong to Jesus, and he loves us just as we are. We are called to respond to the love of Jesus in our lives. Jesus is here with us in our hearts, our lives, our world, and beyond. The love of Jesus Christ for us lasts forever.

HAVE A PRAISE PARADE FOR JESUS

Invite children to celebrate Jesus' love for them with a praise parade. Play an upbeat children's song. Pick a song with a refrain that is easy to sing so all the children can join in.

Children can clap their hands or play a variety of children's instruments such as tambourines or wrist bells. Rhythm sticks can be made by cutting wooden dowels into pieces. Children then tap two sticks together in time to the music.

While the music plays, the children walk in a line around the space where you gather—and outside if weather permits. Encourage children to sing and use their instruments to praise Jesus for the love he has for each of us.

PRAY ALWAYS

Prayer starter » *Jesus, thank you for...*

Share your love prayer » *Lord Jesus, we know that we belong to you. Open our hearts to your love in our lives. Help us remember that you will always love us. We do not have to earn your love, because you give it to us freely. By our words and actions, may we be a sign of your love for others. Guide our lives so that we may walk with you always. Amen.*

Jesus calls us to follow him

EXPLORE THE MESSAGE

Just as he called his first disciples, Jesus calls each of us to follow him. Encourage children to listen for the call of Jesus in their lives.

Jesus said to them, "Follow me."

» MARK 1:17

These words of Jesus echo through the years. Jesus speaks to our hearts and lives today. We are called to follow him and live as his disciples. The Holy Spirit will help us follow in the footsteps of Christ.

We encounter Jesus:

- in our hearts,
- through other people,
- in the gospels,
- when we pray,
- at Mass,
- in the sacraments,
- through serving others,
- in sharing the good news.

Each day we are called to live as disciples of Jesus. We give praise to Jesus. We live the gospels through our words and actions toward others. Jesus is here with us in all that we do, and we can always turn to him.

DO A DISCIPLES ECHO PANTOMIME

The catechist goes line by line saying the words and doing the actions. Children echo the words and the gestures.

As Jesus was walking	*walk in place*
he saw Peter and Andrew fishing.	*shade eyes*
Jesus said to them,	*hands by mouth*
"Follow me."	*gesture with arm*
So they left their nets	*push away hands*
and followed him.	*walk in place*
Jesus calls us today	*stretch out arms*
to be his disciples.	*hands on heart*
Jesus shows us the way.	*shake head yes*
to live in love	*hands on heart*
with one another.	*arms out at side*
We are to walk always	*walk in place*
with Jesus our Lord.	*point to palms*

PRAY ALWAYS

Prayer starter » *Jesus, help me to hear your call and...*

Live as disciples prayer » *Jesus, hope of the world, we know you call us to live as your disciples. Help us to hear your call in our lives. Help us become all that we were created to be. May we follow you in what we do each day. Remind us that we never walk alone because you are always with us. Amen.*

Jesus asks us to come and see

EXPLORE THE MESSAGE

In the gospel Jesus calls people to come and see. He invites them to follow him and be his disciples.

Jesus said to them, "Come and see."

» JOHN 1:39

Jesus also calls us to come and see who he is. He invites us to encounter him in our lives, just as the disciples did in theirs. Jesus shows us the way to the Father with the help of the Holy Spirit. Jesus calls us to live as God's creation. Jesus walks with us on our faith journey.

We say yes to Jesus:

- Yes, we will be disciples of Jesus.
- Yes, we will open our hearts to others.
- Yes, we will follow Jesus in all things.

In following Jesus we become all that we can be. Each of us is someone special who has been chosen by God. Jesus calls us to come and see the possibilities in our lives. We follow his way of love for all people. We will never be alone, because we walk with Jesus through this life and beyond.

MAKE A WALK WITH JESUS PLEDGE

Talk with the children about ways to follow Jesus. Encourage children to contribute their ideas. Explore ideas and encourage children to give specific examples.

How to walk with Jesus:

- Love other people.
- Live in peace.
- Help the poor.
- Forgive others.
- Pray each day.

Make a pledge form for each child to fill out with how he or she will walk with Jesus. Put the title "Walk with Jesus" at the top of a half sheet of paper. Then print "I will walk with Jesus by..." and add a line for the child to put what he or she will do. Add a shorter line near the bottom for the child's name. Add a cross on the left side. Duplicate two to a page.

Each child gets a pledge to fill out. This helps personalize the idea of walking with Jesus. It reminds children that each of us is called by Jesus to follow him. We invite children to hear that call and answer it in their lives.

PRAY ALWAYS

Prayer starter » *Jesus, I know that I am never alone because...*

Come and see prayer » *Jesus, Savior of all people, we ask you to bless us this day. Help us to say yes to you in our lives. Show us how to come and see who you really are. Guide us to live as your disciples with love for you and for all people. Amen.*

Jesus chooses us to be his disciples

EXPLORE THE MESSAGE

Jesus calls us to follow him and be his disciples. Jesus called his first disciples, and he calls us today. This call comes to each one of us. Each of us encounters Jesus in our life. We must respond to his call and live as his disciples.

Jesus called his disciples and chose twelve of them.

» LUKE 6:13

We open our hearts to hear the call of Jesus. Jesus has chosen each of us to be his disciple. Encourage children to walk the way of Jesus. We sign ourselves with the cross as a sign of our faith in Jesus Christ.

What the cross means to us:

- Jesus loves us.
- Jesus came for all people.
- Jesus calls us to be his disciples.
- Jesus brings us new life.
- Jesus shows us the way.

God has created each of us for a purpose. By following the way of Jesus, we find meaning for our lives. Jesus gives each of us special gifts and talents that we can use to help others. Walking with Jesus is an adventure. It can lead us places we never expected. Jesus helps us be all that we can be.

CREATE A JEWELED CROSS

The cross reminds us to live as disciples of Jesus each day. Help each of the children create a colorful cross of their own. Use foam crosses, peel and stick craft foam, self-stick jewels, and scissors.

To make a jeweled cross, each child selects a foam cross. Then they cut seven colorful squares from self-stick craft foam. Children peel off the backing and place five squares down the middle and two across. Then they place a self-stick jewel in the middle of each square. Assist children as needed. Ask the children to display their cross at home to remember that Jesus calls us to follow him each day.

PRAY ALWAYS

Prayer starter » *Jesus, may I hear your call and...*

Prayer to Jesus » *Jesus, Lord of all people, thank you for calling us to be your disciples and for your love for each of us. We praise you for all that you have done for us. Help us to walk in faith and follow your way of love in all that we do. Amen.*

Jesus is with us always

EXPLORE THE MESSAGE

Jesus loves us with an unending love. Jesus is with us at all times and places. We are never alone. Jesus will never turn away from us. We can count on Jesus.

Jesus said to his disciples, "And remember, I am with you always."

» MATTHEW 28:20

Jesus makes this promise to all his disciples, including us. We can have faith in Jesus, who loved us even to the cross. We are called into a relationship with Jesus and with other people. We must trust in Jesus in good times and in bad. We are to be people who hope in Jesus always.

Encourage children to look for ways that Jesus is in their lives. Let children know that being disciples of Jesus does not mean that the way will be easy but rather that Jesus will be with us through it all. We must let the light of Jesus shine in our hearts and our lives. In what we say and do we can bring the light of Christ to others.

BRAINSTORM IDEAS

Help children think about what it means to say Jesus is always with us. Give examples, and encourage children to contribute their own ideas. Let shy children learn from listening to others.

Jesus is with us:

- at home with family,
- when we're with friends,
- in times of sadness,
- when we are afraid,
- when we try something new,
- at school,
- if we are sick,
- at Mass,
- when we are happy,
- when we pray.

Explore with children the idea that Jesus always walks with us no matter where we are or what we are doing. We know that Jesus will never leave us. Remind children that we don't have to earn the love of Jesus. God—Father, Son, and Holy Spirit—created us out of love and will love us always.

PRAY ALWAYS

Prayer starter » *Jesus, help me to know you are with me when...*

Faith in Jesus prayer » *Jesus, we know that you are with us in all things. Guide us to have faith in you always. May we remember that you walk with us each day in the happy times and in the sad times. Thank you for being with us in our hearts and in our lives. Amen.*

CHAPTER 2

Encounter Jesus in other people

Jesus showed God's love for all people through his actions. He took time for individual people even when so many people wanted to see him. He healed the sick, the blind, and the lame. He welcomed those who were outcasts. Jesus shows us what the kingdom of God is all about.

Share with children that everyone is important in God's kingdom. No person's life is worth more than the life of another person. We too are called to bring healing to the lives of others. We need to be aware of people who need our help.

We can bring comfort to people who are sick, injured, in the hospital, grieving, homebound, poor, or treated as outcasts. We can make a difference one person at a time. We encounter Jesus in the faces of other people when we are people of compassion.

We walk with other people on our journey with Jesus. As disciples of Jesus we are called to be people who care about other people in his name.

Jesus helps us reach out

EXPLORE THE MESSAGE

Jesus loves each of us. We are all important to Jesus. He shows this to people in the gospels by his words and his actions. Everything Jesus did, he did with love. We are called to share the love of Jesus with others.

Jesus said to the crowd, "In everything do to others as you would have them do to you." » MATTHEW 7:12

Jesus reached out to the poor and people treated as outcasts. He helped the sick and people who were ignored by others. Remind the children that Jesus calls us to help other people.

Ways to reach out to others:

- Say something kind to another person.
- Help a person who is elderly.
- Share what you have with those who have less.
- Treat all people with respect.
- Encourage someone who is sad.
- Show the love of Jesus to others.

We were created to live in a community with others. As we walk with Jesus, we must look for opportunities to help other people. We need to take time for others even when we would rather be doing something else. We are to reach out a helping hand in Jesus' name.

TALK ABOUT SCENARIOS

It is important to teach children to have empathy for others. They learn this by putting themselves in someone's place. We must help them understand that we are to have compassion for people in difficult situations, just as Jesus did.

Ask children what it would feel like to be the person in the scenarios that follow. See if they understand if a person would be sad, afraid, embarrassed, afraid, lonely, or hurting.

- A new child has no one to play with at recess.
- Someone trips at school and other kids laugh.
- A younger kid is shoved by older kids in the hallway.
- Your classmate did not do well on a test.
- Someone calls another child a dummy.
- A child in your class broke his arm and has a cast.
- One of your parents looks very tired.
- Your sister wasn't invited to a party.
- You see an elderly person using a walker.

Remind children that Jesus wants us to reach out to people in need. We were created to help one another on our journey through this life. We should notice when someone needs help or encouragement. Suggest that children begin with small acts of kindness. Each of us can do something to help other people.

PRAY ALWAYS

Prayer starter » *Jesus, guide me to help others by...*

Love others prayer » *Jesus Christ, Lord and Redeemer, you teach us to love other people with all our hearts. Help us remember to treat other people like we would like to be treated. Show us how to share your love with others and reach out with a helping hand to people in need. Amen.*

Jesus teaches us to have compassion

EXPLORE THE MESSAGE

Through his actions, Jesus shows how much God loves us. Jesus had great compassion for people, especially the sick. He healed people including those who were blind or couldn't walk.

Jesus said to him, "Stand up, take your mat and walk." At once the man was made well.

» JOHN 5:8–9

We are called to be like Jesus and care about others. Jesus was never too busy to listen to people who came to him. Time after time in the gospels we see how Jesus stopped what he was doing to reach out to someone in need. We are to make time for the needs of other people too.

Follow the example of Jesus:

- Jesus brought hope to others.
- Jesus took time to listen to people.
- Jesus did not judge people.
- Jesus helped the sick.
- Jesus made people's lives better.

We encounter Jesus when we have compassion for other people. We must pay attention to the lives of others and not just our own. We can bring hope to the lives of others by our actions. Jesus shows us the way.

PUT UP A KINDNESS TREE

Show children ways they can care about others by helping people around them. As disciples of Jesus we are called to be people of mercy, compassion, and kindness toward others.

Before gathering with the children, put a large paper tree on a bulletin board. Cut out a brown rectangle for the trunk and top it with a large bumpy green circle. Staple the pieces to the bulletin board. Label it "Our Kindness Tree."

Remind the children that Jesus calls us to help others. Talk with children about acts of kindness they will do for someone else.

Acts of kindness:

- Hold the door for an elderly person.
- Play a game with a younger child.
- Make a card for someone who is sick.
- Accompany a parent in visiting someone in assisted living.
- Say hello to a new child in your class.

Encourage each child to print on a hand shape one of the ways they will be kind to others. They can use just a few words. Attach these hand shapes as "leaves" to the tree.

PRAY ALWAYS

Prayer starter » *Jesus, help me to show compassion by...*

Open our hearts prayer » *Jesus, Savior of the world, open our hearts to people who need our help. Teach us compassion for others. Strengthen us to put our faith into action and live in love each day. Be with us so that we may follow you and reach out to others with kindness. Amen.*

Jesus teaches us to care about the sick

EXPLORE THE MESSAGE

The gospels are full of stories of how Jesus had compassion for people who were sick. He helped people who came to him. When a man with leprosy asks Jesus to heal him, Jesus does just that.

Then Jesus stretched out his hand, touched him, and said, "I do choose. Be made clean." Immediately the leprosy left him.

» LUKE 5:13

What a miracle this was for the person with leprosy. He would have been kept away from his family and friends because of his disease. Because Jesus healed him, the person's life was changed forever, and he could go home.

Jesus calls us to reach out to people who are sick in our communities and our world. Jesus opens our hearts to the needs of others. As disciples of Jesus we are to see the face of Jesus in other people. We encounter Jesus when we reach out a helping hand to people who are sick.

MAKE A LIST

Guide children as they discover there are many ways we can show care for people who are injured, ill, elderly, or homebound. Invite children to share ideas. Write their ideas on a white board. It helps children to see as well as hear the ideas. Include suggestions you have too.

Ways to care for the sick:

- Create a get-well card for someone who is sick.
- Go with your family to visit an elderly neighbor.
- Make an activity box for a child in the hospital.

- Put together heart tray favors for residents in a nursing home.
- Help with a parish projects for the sick or elderly.

Ask children to choose a way to help the sick this week. This could be an idea they discussed or their own idea. Let children know that it brings hope and healing to others when people care. Each of us can make a difference.

PRAY ALWAYS

Prayer starter » *Jesus, help me reach out to the sick by...*

Prayer for the sick » *Loving Jesus, healer of the sick, we pray for all those who are sick in our families, our community, and our world. Help people who are sick to know that you are always with them. Guide us to bring comfort to the lives of others with our words and our caring hearts. May we show love and care to sick people as you did. Amen.*

Jesus calls us to rejoice

EXPLORE THE MESSAGE

Jesus teaches his disciples that we are to follow his way of love and rejoice in him. Jesus shows us how to live the life for which we were created. We are to put God first in our lives and love others as God loves us.

Jesus taught them, saying, "Rejoice and be glad."

» MATTHEW 5:12

It brings joy and peace to our hearts to live as Jesus teaches us. As disciples of Jesus we are to share with others the joy that Jesus brings. We can do this by telling others about Jesus.

We encounter Jesus in reaching out to others as he did. Jesus is present with us in all that we do. The Holy Spirit helps each of us to live as

Jesus teaches us. Jesus shows us the way to the Father, and for that we rejoice.

GIVE OUT POSITIVE POSTCARDS

We are called to share the joy of Jesus Christ with others in our lives. At home, at school, and wherever we go, we can look for opportunities to be caring people. Our words make a difference. We should choose positive things to say to encourage other people, rather than words of criticism. Our words can bring hope and healing to the lives of others.

A fun way for children to share kind words with others is with positive postcards. Before gathering with the children, run off messages of encouragement on cardstock, four to a page. Then cut apart.

Positive postcard messages:

- Have a terrific day!
- Remember Jesus loves you!
- Welcome to our school!
- Thank you for all you do!
- You have a great smile!
- Jesus is always with you!
- You are a great friend!

Ask the children to decorate the postcards with colorful markers or stickers. These positive messages bring joy to the lives of others. Encourage children to put the postcards where others will find them, such as on a family member's pillow or another child's desk. Ask children how they think a person will feel when they receive a postcard. Small things can make a difference in the lives of others.

PRAY ALWAYS

Prayer starter » *Jesus, may I share my joy in you by...*

Joy prayer » *Jesus, light of the world, we rejoice in your love for each of us. Show us how to live in joy and bring joy to the lives of others. May we share the good news of your love with other people. Send your Holy Spirit to show us how to be your disciples each day. Amen.*

Jesus teaches us to love others

EXPLORE THE MESSAGE

Jesus calls us to love God and love others. This is called the great commandment. We created to live in a community and help one another.

Jesus answered, "Love your neighbor as yourself."

» MARK 12:31

These words speak to how we are to live today. We are called to love others, as Jesus teaches us. We are to reach out and help others even when we will not be thanked or appreciated. We are called to show other people the love of Jesus by our actions. In loving others we encounter Jesus Christ in our lives.

We remember:

- Jesus came for people of all races and all nations.
- We are to live as Jesus shows us with love for all people.
- Jesus calls us to reach out to others with kindness and compassion.
- We should not to limit our loving actions only to those who thank us.
- People learn about the love Jesus has for them through us.

Jesus came for all people. Even those who nailed him to a cross. We are to love others as Jesus did. This is a challenge, but with Jesus all things are possible.

CREATE FINGERPRINT HEARTS

Remind the children that Jesus teaches us to love others. Jesus shows us what this means by his word and actions. Because we love Jesus, we are called to love other people too.

Show children how to make a unique fingerprint hearts to remember to love others. Before gathering with the children, draw a large heart on the left side of a piece of paper and put the words "Love others" on the right. Duplicate for each child.

The children then create fingerprint hearts. Explain that each heart will be different because each of us has different fingerprints. Each child touches a finger to a colorful ink pad and then inside his or her fingerprint heart. Have them use several colors until their heart is filled with colorful fingerprints. Remind children that Jesus calls each of us to love others. Children take home their heart to share with their family.

PRAY ALWAYS

Prayer starter » *Jesus, open my heart to love others by...*

Walk with Jesus prayer » *Jesus, Lord of all people, teach us to walk with you and love others as you did. Show us how to take the time to reach out to other people. May we offer a smile, a kind word, or a helping hand to at least one person today. Amen.*

CHAPTER 3

Encounter Jesus in prayer

Jesus shows us by his example that prayer is important. Jesus prayed before all his big decisions. We are to be people of prayer in all that we do. Prayer is important in our relationship with Jesus. We encounter Jesus in our lives through prayer. Our prayers connect us with Jesus.

Prayer helps us celebrate that we walk with Jesus and he is here with us. Prayer strengthens us as we reach out to Jesus and follow his way. Through prayer we learn who we were created to be. Sometimes life is difficult, and only a lot of prayer gets us through.

One of the important things that we do as catechists, teachers, and families is to help children learn to pray in all things. By praying with the children, they learn to pray. We should also pray for the children entrusted to us.

Show children how to pray in a variety of ways so that they are able to find ways that speak to their hearts and their lives. Children should know traditional prayers that allow us to pray together and also be able to pray to Jesus in their own words. As disciples of Jesus we are to pray for the needs of other people. We guide children to do this by making prayer for others part of our time together.

Jesus teaches us to pray

EXPLORE THE MESSAGE

Jesus always took time for prayer. The gospels show many times and places that Jesus prayed.

And after Jesus had dismissed the crowds,
he went up the mountain by himself to pray.

» MATTHEW 14:23

We are called to follow the example of Jesus. Explain to children that prayers connect us with Jesus. We can share our feelings, our hopes, and our dreams with Jesus. He wants to hear about what is important to us.

Prayer helps us to live as disciples each day. Prayer is part of walking with Jesus. Help children discover the many times and places in our lives that we can pray. We can pray in the morning, during the day, at dinner, or before bed. We can pray alone or with others. We can pray at home, at school, or outside. There are many opportunities to pray in our lives.

Let children know that Jesus loves us and wants to be part of our lives. Jesus is waiting for us to turn to him in prayer. Just as we talk with our friends, so we should talk with Jesus about what is going on in our lives. Through prayer we encounter Jesus, who is already here with us.

SHARE WAYS TO PRAY

Talk with the children about a variety of ways to pray. Encourage them to share their own ideas too.

Ways to pray:

- Share with Jesus what is going on in your life.

- Thank Jesus for his love for you.
- Pray to Jesus for help in living as his disciple.
- Ask Jesus to bless your day.
- Pray in your own words.
- Say the Our Father.
- Read the gospels and open your heart to Jesus.
- Go to Mass and pray with others.
- Pray for the needs of other people.

Explore with children the idea that we can make more time for prayer by doing less of something else. We pray because Jesus loves us and is with us in all that we do.

PRAY ALWAYS

Prayer starter » *Jesus, may I follow your example by praying...*

Prayer for courage » *Jesus, Son of God, thank you for coming to show us how to live. Give us the courage to follow you and do what is right and good. Help us to listen to your voice speaking in our lives. Show us how to be people of prayer in all things. Amen.*

Jesus hears our prayers

EXPLORE THE MESSAGE

Jesus shows us that prayer is important by his actions in the gospels. Jesus prayed before making decisions. He prayed before choosing his first disciples.

Jesus spent the night in prayer to God. And when day came, he called his disciples and chose twelve of them.

» LUKE 6:12–13

Prayer is a part of our relationship with Jesus. He wants to hear about what is important to us. In the gospels we see that Jesus prays to the Father. Through all he does, Jesus shows us the love that God has for us. We are called to be people of prayer in our lives as Jesus was. Through prayer we encounter Jesus present in our lives today and always.

Prayer is important:

- Prayer is a way we respond to the love of Jesus.
- We encounter Jesus in our lives when we pray.
- Prayer shows us who Jesus is and who we are as his disciples.
- We are to make prayer a part of our lives each day.
- Jesus will always hear our prayers.

Like Jesus, we should pray before making decisions. Prayer reminds us of what is important in life. Let's be people of prayer in all we do. Reassure children that if they turn to Jesus in prayer and no words will come, that is all right. Jesus will hear the prayers in their hearts.

USE PRAYER PROMPTS

One way to pray is by using prayer prompts. This activity helps children get started in praying in their own words.

Prayer prompts:

- Thank Jesus for always loving you.
- Pray to Jesus to help you in difficult times.
- Give thanks to Jesus for giving you new life.
- Pray to Jesus to fill your heart with love for others.
- Ask Jesus to be with you in all things.
- Pray to Jesus to help people who are sick.
- Give praise to Jesus for the people who care about you.
- Ask Jesus to open your hearts to the needs of others.

Share with children that prayers do not have to be long. Even a prayer of a few words helps us encounter Jesus, who is always here in our lives.

PRAY ALWAYS

Prayer starter » *Jesus, remind me to pray...*

Example prayer » *Jesus, Lord and Savior, help us to learn from your example of prayer. We know that prayer is important in our lives and in our relationship with you. Thank you for hearing our prayers. Show us how to pray in all that we do each day. In this way we live always as your disciples. Amen.*

Jesus calls us to pray

EXPLORE THE MESSAGE

The gospels show us that Jesus was a person of prayer in all things. Jesus started his day with prayer in the morning.

In the morning, while it was still very dark, Jesus got up and went out to a deserted place, and there he prayed.

» MARK 1:35

We too can pray in the morning. We should offer each day to Jesus. We can do this before we even get out of bed in the morning. We can also find moments during the day to give thanks to Jesus for his love. We can ask Jesus to show us the way. Jesus hears our prayers.

TAKE HOME JESUS PRAYER CARDS

We are called to be people of prayer each day. One way to encourage children to pray to Jesus is by giving them prayer cards to take home. Print off the short prayers below that speak to the children's experience of Jesus. Add a cross to each prayer card and copy four to a page. Cut apart and put the prayer cards in a basket. Ask each child to choose one to take home.

Lord Jesus, thank you for loving me
with an unending love. Guide me
to share your love with others. Amen.

Jesus, Savior of the world, I give you thanks
for all you have done for me. Help me
to follow you in all I do and say. Amen.

Jesus, Lord of mercy, show me
your way of love so that I may
walk with you today and always. Amen.

Jesus, servant of all, open my heart
to the needs of other people. Help me
to serve others as you did. Amen.

Lord Jesus, you are the light of the world.
May I walk in your light and bring hope
to the lives of others. Amen.

Children can share their prayer cards with their families.

PRAY ALWAYS

Prayer starter » *Jesus, show me how to walk in your light by...*

Hear us prayer » *Jesus, hope of all people, help us to give glory to you by our prayers and by the way we live each day. We know that you are the way to the Father and to new life. Hear the prayers we offer to you today and the prayers unsaid in our hearts. Amen.*

Jesus prays for us

EXPLORE THE MESSAGE

Jesus shows us how to be a people of prayer in all things. On the night before he died, Jesus prayed for his disciples and for all of us.

Jesus prayed, "I ask not only on behalf of these, but also on behalf of those who will believe in me through their word, that all shall be one."

» JOHN 17:20–21

As disciples of Jesus, we are called to pray for the needs of others as he did. Praying for others is part of our relationship with Jesus and with one another. Prayer is not just words we say. Prayer is an action word. We are not only to pray but to put our prayers into action as Jesus did.

Ways to put prayers into action:

- We pray for the hungry...and we give food to the parish food pantry.
- We pray for the sick...and we bring new toys to a children's hospital.
- We pray for people in poverty...and we donate to Catholic Relief Services.
- We thank God for sending Jesus...and we share the good news with others.

Remind children that in prayer we encounter Jesus Christ who is here with us. We were created to help one another on this faith journey. We may be the answer to someone's prayers.

ASSEMBLE A PRAYER BOWL

We follow the example of Jesus in being people who pray for the needs of others. A prayer bowl activity helps children learn to pray for people such as those who are hungry, sick, refugees, homebound, poor, and others.

- Write down people for whom to pray on 2" x 4" pieces of colored paper.
- Fold each paper in half, and put all of them in a bowl.
- Ask each child to take a slip of paper from the bowl.
- Begin by asking Jesus to hear our prayers.
- Each child reads what is on their paper such as, "We pray for the sick."
- Children respond to each one, "Lord, hear our prayer."
- Close by asking for God's blessing on all people in need in our world.

This activity involves the children in praying for others. Encourage children to continue to pray for people in need in our world. Encourage families to do this type of activity at home.

PRAY ALWAYS

Prayer starter • *Jesus, I pray for...*

Prayer for others • *Jesus, light of all nations, thank you for your love and for showing us the way to the Father. Help us to live your way of love. Open our eyes to the needs of others. Guide us to pray not only for ourselves but for the needs of other people. May we walk always in your light. Amen.*

Jesus gives us the Eucharist

EXPLORE THE MESSAGE

We encounter Jesus Christ in all the sacraments. This is true in a special way in the Eucharist, which is his Body and Blood through the action of the Holy Spirit. Jesus gave us this wonderful gift the night before he died on the cross.

Jesus said, "Take, eat; this is my body...this is my blood."

» MATTHEW 26:26–28

The Eucharist is a sacrament of joy and hope. The Eucharist is an amazing gift given to us by Jesus because he loves us. In the Eucharist Jesus is always with us.

Through the Eucharist we are united with one another. The Eucharist commits us to live as Jesus Christ did—with love for all. We are to treat others as Jesus did. We are to be disciples of Jesus each day and share the good news with other people.

Receiving Jesus in this sacrament should make a difference in our lives. The Eucharist strengthens us for our faith journey. We then go out to serve others in the name of Jesus.

LIVE AS JESUS SHOWS US

When we share in the Eucharist, we commit ourselves to living as Jesus lived. We are united with others through this sacrament. We are to live as people of the Eucharist.

Explore what this means with questions.

- How can we serve people in need in our community?
- Why do we value people of all races?
- How can we use our God-given gifts to help other people?

- What are ways to be peacemakers in our own lives?
- How do we show the love of Jesus by our words and actions?

The Eucharist is so important in our lives. Celebrating the Eucharist together helps us live as disciples in all that we do. It gives us strength for our journey with Jesus.

PRAY ALWAYS

Prayer starter » *Jesus, may I witness to your love by...*

Give us strength prayer » *Lord Jesus Christ, bread of life, you give us the amazing gift of yourself in the Eucharist. You bring joy and hope to our lives. May our celebration of the Eucharist give us the strength to be like your disciples in all that we do. Guide us to live as people of the Eucharist each day. Amen.*

CHAPTER 4

Encounter Jesus in the gospels

We are to live the gospel and share it with others. The gospels are the story of Jesus Christ who came to fulfill God's promise to the people. Jesus redeemed us and brought us new life through his life, death, and resurrection.

Jesus shows us how much God loves us. Through the Holy Spirit, the Bible was written down and handed on from generation to generation in the church. The words of the Bible speak to our lives today.

We encounter Jesus Christ when we hear his word proclaimed. Jesus speaks to us today through the words of the gospels. We must open our hearts to what Jesus wants to teach us. God has an unending love for all people. Jesus calls us to share that love with others. As we explore the four gospels, we learn to walk with Jesus and live as his disciples.

It is important to share the gospels with the next generation. Children need to be familiar with the gospels in order to live as gospel people. Jesus teaches us by his words and actions. Stress to children that we are called to live as Jesus Christ shows us. He is the way, the truth, and the life.

Jesus teaches us to trust

EXPLORE THE MESSAGE

One day Jesus and his disciples were in a boat when a terrible storm came up. Jesus was asleep, but the disciples were afraid the boat would sink. They woke up Jesus.

Jesus said to his disciples, "Why are you afraid? Have you still no faith?"

» MARK 4:40

Then Jesus calmed the storm. The disciples were amazed that he could do this. Jesus is with us too when we face storms and challenges in our lives. This doesn't mean that bad things won't happen to us. It means that Jesus is always with us.

We are to trust Jesus in all the times and places of our lives. We have hope in Jesus Christ our Lord. He will be with us through it all. We can pray to Jesus when we are afraid. We are never alone because Jesus is here! We can count on Jesus.

DO A STORM ECHO PANTOMIME

The gospel story about the storm reminds children and all of us that we can trust in Jesus. Do an echo pantomime of the storm story from Mark 4:35–41.

The catechist or teacher says each line and does the motions. The children echo the words and gestures line by line.

Jesus said to his disciples,	*hands by mouth*
"Let's cross to the other side."	*point ahead*
So they went in a boat.	*pretend to row*
A storm came up	*hands crossed by face*
and waves were coming over the boat.	*rock back and forth*

Jesus was asleep.	*fold hands by head*
The disciples woke him and said,	*hands by mouth*
"Teacher, don't you care?"	*palms up*
Jesus stopped the wind,	*move hand left to right*
and said to the seas, "Quiet! Be still."	*hands next to mouth*
The wind stopped and it was calm.	*finger by mouth*
Jesus asked, "Why are you afraid?"	*palms up*
Do you not yet have faith in me?"	*hands over heart*

The story of Jesus calming the story shows us that Jesus can do anything. We can always trust in Jesus!

PRAY ALWAYS

Prayer starter » *Jesus, be with me...*

Share hope prayer » *Lord Jesus, source of all hope, we know that you are with us always. You love us with an unending love. Help us to put our trust in you even when we face difficult times in our lives. Give us hearts filled with hope, and show us how to share hope in you with others. Amen.*

Jesus calls children

EXPLORE THE MESSAGE

Jesus cares about children. In the gospel we hear how people were bringing children to see Jesus. The disciples asked them to stop. But Jesus loves children and tells the disciples to let the children come to him.

Jesus said, "Let the little children come to me."

» MATTHEW 19:14

This is a wonderful story to share with children (Matthew 19:13–15). This gospel shows that children are important to Jesus. Children need to know that Jesus loves them. Only then can they respond to that love in their lives.

Children are called to be disciples too—right now at whatever age they are. Children have a great capacity to love Jesus and others. We must help children hear Jesus calling them to follow him. Explore ways that we can live as disciples of Jesus Christ.

Ways to answer Jesus' call:

- Put Jesus first in our lives.
- Love others.
- Serve others like Jesus did.
- Pray each day.
- Help people in need.

PLAY A WORDS OF JESUS GAME

Stress to the children that Jesus Christ calls them to follow him. We encounter Jesus when we hear Scripture proclaimed. We are to live as gospel people. Play a game with words of Jesus to learn more about what Jesus teaches us.

If your room doesn't have a white board, get a small dry erase board and marker. Make a dash for each letter in each word of the verse. Leave space between words. Let children take turns guessing letters. Fill in the letters as they are guessed correctly. Children get a chance to guess the phrase when they choose a correct letter. (The chapter and verse is given below for your information.)

Words of Jesus:

- I am with you always. (Matthew 28:20)
- For God all things are possible. (Mark 10:27)
- Proclaim the good news. (Mark 16:15)
- Forgive and you will be forgiven. (Luke 6:37)
- Love the Lord your God with all your heart. (Luke 10:27)
- Love one another as I have loved you. (John 15:12)

This game can be played by individuals or teams. Give hints if needed.

PRAY ALWAYS

Prayer starter » *Jesus, help me to live the gospels by...*

Prayer for children » *Lord Jesus Christ, show us how to live as your children. We know that you care about us and love us with an unending love. Help us learn about your words in the gospels so we can live as your disciples. Renew our hearts and our lives so that we may live in your love. Amen.*

Jesus watches over us

EXPLORE THE MESSAGE

In the gospels Jesus tells us that he is the Good Shepherd. The people of Jesus' time would have known about the work of shepherds. The shepherd leads the sheep, stays with them all night, and keeps them safe.

Jesus says to the people "I am the good shepherd and I know mine and mine know me."

» JOHN 10:14

Jesus gives us this example so we would know how much he cares for us. We are the sheep of Jesus' flock. He watches over us. We know his voice.

Jesus is the Good Shepherd:

- Jesus calls us to follow him.
- Jesus wants to keep us safe.
- Jesus knows each one of us.
- Jesus is with us always.
- Jesus wants to bring all of us together.

As a shepherd gathers all the sheep, so Jesus gathers us in. He leads us where we need to go. He loves each of us. We can trust in Jesus always.

LISTEN TO A MEDITATION

Guide children in understanding the story of the Good Shepherd with a children's meditation. Ask the children to put themselves in this gospel story. Children close their eyes or put their heads on their arms as they listen.

> One day Jesus is teaching the people. You are there too, standing at the back of the crowd. Jesus reminds the people that the shepherd calls his sheep by name and leads them. You know someone who is a shepherd, and he works hard taking care of the sheep day and night.
>
> Jesus tells the people that he is the Good Shepherd. Jesus says he knows his sheep and they know him. He will not leave them He will give his life for his sheep. You realize that Jesus isn't really talking about sheep; he is talking about people. You see Jesus look at you. You know he cares about you and will be with you.
>
> Because Jesus is the Good Shepherd, he watches over us. Then Jesus says that he will bring in other sheep so there will be one flock, one shepherd. You realize that Jesus came for all people. You are happy that all of us belong to Jesus. Come back now to this time and place as we pray together.

PRAY ALWAYS

Prayer starter » *Jesus, may I follow you always in...*

Good Shepherd prayer » *Jesus, Good Shepherd of all people, thank you for your love and for watching over us. We know that you are always with us and will never leave us alone. You take care of us and keep us safe. You* *know each of us by name. May we always trust in you and follow where you lead us. Amen.*

Jesus challenges us to have mercy

EXPLORE THE MESSAGE

In the Gospel of Luke, Jesus answers a question with a story about the good Samaritan. He wants people to understand that we are to have mercy on other people. Jesus calls us to care about all people.

Then Jesus tells the lawyer, "Go and do likewise."

» LUKE 10:37

Read this story to your group from a children's Bible (Luke 10:25–37). This is a story for all ages. Explain that some people looked down on the Samaritan people. They would not expect a Samaritan to show mercy to the injured traveler.

Jesus challenges his listeners to look at things a different way. We are to share the love of Jesus with others. We are to help even those who cannot or will not pay us back. This story speaks to our lives today. We can see the wounded traveler in people such as the homeless, victims of violence, refugees, and others. We are to be the good Samaritan for other people.

ACT OUT GOSPEL CHARADES

It is important for children to be familiar with the gospels that we are to live. In the gospels we encounter Jesus today as the people did in Jesus' time. A fun way to review gospel stories is with a game of gospel charades. Before gathering with the children print gospel story titles on slips of paper and put them in a basket.

Divide children into groups of three or more. Let someone from the first group draw a slip of paper from the basket. Briefly take that group aside. Give them a quick overview of the gospel story and some simple ideas for acting out the story without using words.

Gospel stories to act out:

- Call of the disciples (Matthew 4:18–22)
- Jesus calms the storm (Mark 4:35–41)
- Jesus and the children (Mark 10:13–16)
- Blind man sees (Mark 10:46–52)
- Prodigal son (Luke 15:11–32)

The other children watch the gospel story being acted out and then guess which story it is. Give hints as needed. Then let other groups have their turn. Everyone gets to participate.

PRAY ALWAYS

Prayer starter » *Jesus, guide me to show mercy to others by...*

Live the gospel prayer » *Jesus, Savior of all people, show us how to live the gospels and be people of mercy. Open our hearts to the needs of others. Teach us to love one another. Give us the courage to do what is right. May we treat all people with dignity and respect in your name. Amen.*

Jesus is the way

EXPLORE THE MESSAGE

We are to follow Jesus as his disciples in all that we do. Jesus came to redeem us and show us the way to the Father.

Jesus says to Thomas, "I am the way and the truth and the life."

» JOHN 14:6

Jesus teaches us that God has an unending love for each of us. We are to follow Jesus. He shows us the way. Jesus helps us become who God created us to be from the beginning. Each of us has a special purpose in life.

Follow the way of Jesus Christ:

- Answer the call of Jesus.
- Live the gospels in our lives.
- Have a relationship with Jesus our Savior.
- Love other people in what we say and do.
- Share hope in Jesus and hope in the future.

We encounter Jesus in our lives, in the gospels, and in one another. On our faith journey we walk the way of Jesus together. We help one another follow Jesus in all that we do.

DECORATE A FRAME CRAFT

This is a simple craft that helps children remember to follow the way of Jesus. Before gathering with the children, run off copies of the words "I am the way and the truth and the life" (John 14:16). Also assemble glue sticks, colorful foam craft frames, and foam stickers such as crosses, hearts, and foot shapes.

When the children come together, talk about how we are to follow the way of Jesus. Remind the children that Jesus came for each one of us. Then let children make a "Jesus is the way" frame craft. Show children how to glue the gospel verse to the back of the frame. Next they decorate the frame with stickers.

This craft is a reminder to follow Jesus in our lives. Jesus is the way, the truth, and the life for each of us. Jesus is always here with us and shows us the way to the Father. Sharing the craft with their families extends learning into the children's lives.

PRAY ALWAYS

Prayer starter » *Jesus, give me the courage to…*

Way, truth, and life prayer » *Lord Jesus, we ask you to be with us each day. We know that you are the way and the truth and the life. Guide our lives that we may walk always as your disciples. Give us the strength to witness to who you are by how we live each day. May we remember that you are with us always. Amen.*

CHAPTER 5

Encounter Jesus in serving others

Jesus wants us to serve others, just as he was the servant of all. As individuals, and together, we can make a difference in the lives of others. God gives us many gifts and wants us to share them with others. We were created to live as a community of God's people. We are to take care of one another. We are all on this faith journey together.

Jesus shows us what it means to live a life of service. He always had time for people. He never told them to go away because he was busy. We too are to make time for the needs of other people.

Explore with children the idea that we encounter Jesus when we reach out to others, especially people in need. We must be aware of the needs of others and think of ways to help them. Each of us can make a difference. The key is to love Jesus and to love one another.

As catechists, as teachers, as families, we show children by our words and especially by our example what it means to serve others. In living as disciples, we are called to follow in Jesus' footsteps and walk in his way.

Jesus teaches us to give

EXPLORE THE MESSAGE

Jesus asks us to share what we have with others. This has been God's plan for us from the beginning. The resources of our world are meant to be shared with all.

Jesus says to Peter, "From everyone to whom much has been given, much will be required."

» LUKE 12:48

In what he said and did, Jesus shows us what it means to give to others. We are to see Jesus in one another. We encounter Jesus in the lives of other people. God created us to live as community and help one another.

We are called to serve others in the name of Jesus. We must reach out to those living in poverty, people treated as outcasts, the elderly, refugees, the sick, homebound, and others who need our help. We may be the answer to someone's prayers.

We need to be aware of the needs of other people. We can help people in need in our local community. Stress to the children in your group that each of us can make a difference in the life of someone else.

DRAW A CARING PICTURE

Explain to the children that we can help people around us. Talk with the children about ways to show love and kindness to other people. Encourage children to share their own ideas.

Ways to care:

- Ask a new child to sit by you at lunch.
- Make a get-well card for someone in the hospital.
- Donate new stuffed animals to the fire department.

- Say something nice to a person who seems lonely.
- Go with your family to visit someone in a care center.

Ask children to draw a picture of themselves helping someone. This personalizes the idea of giving for children. They have to think of an idea before they can draw it. Provide paper and markers for this project. When they are finished, invite children to share their pictures with the whole group.

PRAY ALWAYS

Prayer starter » *Jesus, teach me to follow in your footsteps by...*

Prayer to help other people » *Lord of all nations, we thank you for being with us. Help us share the resources of our world with others. May we reach out to other people with kindness and compassion as you did. Help us to pray for the needs of others too. Send your Holy Spirit to renew our hearts and our lives. Amen.*

Jesus tells us to love one another

EXPLORE THE MESSAGE

We are to live as Jesus' disciples in all things. Jesus tells us to love one another. Having a relationship with Jesus means having a relationship with other people. We are to live what we believe.

Jesus says, "Love one another as I have loved you." » JOHN 15:12

We love others because God created and loves all people. Our actions toward other people show them who Jesus is. They see the love of Jesus through what we say and do. Love is an action word. It means going out of our way to do things for others as Jesus did. We are to see other people as Jesus does.

Jesus teaches us that we were created for life in a community. We encounter Jesus when we love others in his name. We must look out for one another and help others in any way we can. Each day we can find opportunities to be the people God created us to be. We should pray for the needs of other people in our lives and in our world.

MAKE THINKING-OF-YOU CARDS

Children can show love for others by making colorful "thinking of you" cards. Ask children to open their hearts to people in our community who are elderly, homebound, sick, or living in a care center. Explain that some older people may be unable to go places on their own and may have few visitors.

Create colorful cards for:

- elderly people in your parish,
- people in the hospital,
- people who are homebound.
- care center residents,
- meal delivery clients,

Be sure children understand that the greeting is to be "Thinking of you." These are not get-well cards because many of these people may or may not have ongoing health problems. Provide colored paper and markers to make the cards. Ask children to make a card that they think an older person would like.

Remind children to remember elderly people and those who are homebound in their prayers too. This project gives children the opportunity to love one another as Jesus teaches us and gets them started in serving others.

PRAY ALWAYS

Prayer starter » *Jesus, I will walk in love by...*

Reach out prayer » *Jesus, Lord and Savior, we praise you for your unending love for each of us. You teach us about your love by your words and your example. Fill our hearts with your love so we will love others as you love us. May we remember to give a helping hand to people in need in our community. Amen.*

Jesus calls us to share

EXPLORE THE MESSAGE

The gospels are filled with stories of Jesus reaching out to people. The Gospel of Luke is sometimes called the gospel of mercy because so many of the stories show God's mercy and love for all people.

Jesus tells the crowd, "Be merciful just as your Father is merciful."

» LUKE 6:36

Jesus shows us how to live by his words and his actions. We are to follow his example. We are called to share what we have with others, so that they will have what they need to live. Jesus came for all people.

We can share our time, our individual talents, compassion, resources, and love. We are to work for justice in our world. In doing this we encounter Jesus through the lives of other people. We are called to have a relationship with Jesus and with one another. Jesus wants us to bring hope to the lives of others.

SERVE OTHERS WITH A BIRTHDAY PROJECT

Provide an opportunity for children to share with other children in their community. Explain that homeless families living in shelters often do not have money to buy birthday gifts for their children. Collect toys to be used as birthday presents for children living in the local family shelter. (It is important that the toys be new; every child deserves a new toy for their birthday.) Suitable items include puzzle cubes, musical toys, art sets, trucks, dolls, action figures, and card games.

How to do a birthday gift collection:

- Check with the shelter about their needs.
- Send home a note to your families.
- Provide marked boxes to collect the toys.
- Give gifts unwrapped so shelter can match with child.
- Donate gift wrap and birthday cards too.
- Deliver to the shelter.

This is a wonderful way to open our hearts to the needs of children in our local community. It provides an opportunity for children to reach out to children who are experiencing a difficult time in their lives. In this way we share with others as Jesus teaches us. All of us need a helping hand sometime.

PRAY ALWAYS

Prayer starter » *Jesus, guide me to see you in others and...*

Witness prayer » *Jesus, Son of the living God, open our hearts and our eyes to the needs of people around us. Teach us to love others in your name. May we look for opportunities to share your love with others. Guide us to witness to your love for all people by what we say and do. Amen.*

Jesus asks us to serve others

EXPLORE THE MESSAGE

Jesus teaches us by his words and action that we are to serve others. We are called to help other people as Jesus did.

Jesus says to his disciples,
"The greatest among you will be your servant."

» MATTHEW 23:11

Jesus came for all people, all nations, all cultures, and all races. He shows us how people are capable of living. When we serve other people, we serve Jesus. We encounter Jesus in helping other people. Jesus loves all of us.

We are called to serve others:

- All people are created and valued by God.
- Resources of our world are for all of us to share.
- Our gifts and talents are given for good of all.
- We are to see the face of Jesus in other people.
- Our actions can make a difference.

Jesus works with us and through us to serve others. We are to walk in love as his disciples. In serving others we serve Jesus. Encourage children to live in love each day as Jesus did.

MAKE A HELPING HANDS BANNER

Emphasize to children that each of us, regardless of our age, is called to serve others. We are to reach out a helping hand to people in need. Children can make a banner to take home so they will be reminded that Jesus calls us to serve others.

This banner takes only a few supplies, including colored card stock, foam hand shapes, and heart stickers. Also needed are glue, string, and a hole punch. Make copies of the words "Serve others" before gathering with the children.

To make a banner, each child chooses a sheet of colored card stock and punches two holes at the top. They pull string through the holes and knot it to make a hanger. Assist children as needed with tying the knot. Then they glue the words "Serve others" at the top. Children attach a heart sticker to one of the hand shapes and glue the hand shape to the banner

Stress to the children that we are to serve others as Jesus shows us by his words and actions. Encourage children to hang their banner at home where they will see it and be reminded to reach out a helping hand to others.

PRAY ALWAYS

Prayer starter » *Jesus, show me how to reach out to others by...*

Serve others prayer » *Lord Jesus, servant of all, give us hearts filled with love for others. Help us to follow your example in serving other people. We celebrate your presence in our lives and in our world. Enable us to see your face in other people and serve them in your name. Amen.*

Jesus calls us to work together

EXPLORE THE MESSAGE

Jesus loves us and cares about us. In the gospels we hear how Jesus took five loaves and two fish that people shared and made enough food for five thousand people.

Taking the five loaves and two fish, Jesus looked up to heaven, and blessed and broke the loaves and gave them to his disciples to set before the people.

» MARK 6:41

Jesus calls us to share with others too. When Jesus works through us, great things can happen. When people share what they have—such as five loaves and two fish—Jesus can make sure there is enough for all. Read the story of the loaves and fish from the gospels (Mark 6:35–44). Help children understand that we encounter the love of Jesus when we come together to meet the needs of other people.

Connect children's lives with the gospels. Let them know that we can see miracles happen in our own lives when people work together for the benefit of others. We are called as individuals and as a church community to share what we have with others.

HELP A COMMUNITY CLINIC

Stress that we are to serve others as Jesus teaches us. A service project helps children and families help others in the local community. They can collect items for a free medical clinic in your town. Talk with the children about what free clinics do to help people who are sick or injured and unable to pay for medical care.

Neighborhood clinics:

- provide health care at no cost to people who cannot pay,
- help patients who are sick, injured, or have ongoing health issues,
- treat people who might be unable to see a doctor if they had to pay,
- are staffed by volunteer medical professionals and others.

Children know what it is like to be sick and they want to help others who are ill. Encourage children and families to donate supplies. Give a list of needed items, such as rolls of gauze, bandages, gauze pads, adhesive tape, cotton balls, antibiotic cream, and hand sanitizer.

This collection shows that we can make a difference when we work together. It is like the story of the loaves and fish. Jesus took what the people had and made enough for everyone. As more and more people bring in donations, it is amazing to see empty collection boxes get filled with supplies. With Jesus all things are possible.

PRAY ALWAYS

Prayer starter » *Jesus, may I share with others by...*

Give to others prayer » *Lord of love, guide our efforts so that we can work together to bless the lives of other people. Multiply our efforts and our actions so we who have so much can give to others. Open our hearts to work together in your name. May we always remember that you walk with us each day. Amen.*

CHAPTER 6

Encounter Jesus in being peacemakers

We encounter Jesus is our lives when we live in peace with others. We are to accept God's mercy and forgiveness in our lives and share mercy with others. Jesus forgave people, even from the cross. We share with children that we are to witness to the mercy of Jesus by the way we live each day.

Jesus calls us to treat other people with dignity and respect as God's creation. As God's people, we work for peace and justice for all people. We share what we have with others so they will have what they need to survive. We are called to be disciples of hope to others. In the choices we make each day, we walk the way of peace.

Peace is a difficult concept. Forgiveness is too. But children need to hear about these topics from us. We must help children look for the good in one another and in our world. As disciples of Jesus, we are called to work for peace in our world. If we all lived as Jesus teaches us, our world would be transformed.

Jesus brings us peace

EXPLORE THE MESSAGE

After his resurrection, Jesus appeared to the disciples. They had come together in the upper room.

Jesus came and stood among them and said,
"Peace be with you."

» JOHN 20:19

Jesus doesn't say to the disciples, "Why did you run away?" Instead, Jesus offers them peace. Jesus forgives them. Jesus even forgives Peter for denying him three times. Jesus forgives us too. Encountering Jesus means living in peace.

Peace is important:

- Peace is not just stopping violence. It also means making life better for others.
- Peace is accepting our differences and seeing how they enrich our lives.
- Peace doesn't not mean things will go our way. It means our hearts will be at peace because Jesus will be with us.

We should have peace in knowing Jesus Christ is with us. Peace is more than just a good idea. It is how God, who created us and loves us, calls us to live.

WALK IN PEACE IDEAS

We follow the example of Jesus by living in peace with others. We can start with a single person or a single action. Explore with children how sometimes we use our words to hurt others instead of encouraging others as Jesus would. We say "go away" to people, or "that's stupid," or

"Why did you do that?" Saying things like this hurts people's feelings.

Talk about loving words we might say to others, such as "you did a great job," "thanks for all you do," "I like your smile," or "how can I help you?" Ask children to say more positive words to other people. Kind words make others feel better—and us too.

Ways to walk in peace:

- Look for the positive in people and situations.
- Get to know someone who is different from you.
- Stand up for someone being treated unfairly.
- Have the courage to do what is right.
- Pray for peace in our communities and our world.

Ask children to think of other ideas too. Encourage them to look for opportunities to walk in peace. All journeys start with a single step.

PRAY ALWAYS

Prayer starter » *Jesus, show me how to live in peace by...*

Peace prayer » *Lord of peace, you teach us by your word and example what it means to live in peace. We know that you came for all nations and all people. Help us work together for justice and peace in our world. May our words and our actions help bring peace to the lives of other people. Amen.*

Jesus calls us to be peacemakers

EXPLORE THE MESSAGE

Peace is mentioned many times in the gospels. Each of us must work to bring peace to our lives, the lives of others, and our world. It takes all of us working together to make peace a reality.

On the mountain Jesus teaches them,
"Blessed are the peacemakers."

» MATTHEW 5:9

Peace will not come all at once, but each of us can do something. Talk with the children about focusing on one action, one person at a time. Let's all be like Jesus. He did not give up when he looked around and saw all that needed to be done. When we find life difficult, remember that all things are possible with Jesus.

Jesus calls us to be peacemakers in our lives, one act, one word, one person at a time. In this way we begin to be peacemakers. As we live in peace, we encounter Jesus in our lives and the lives of others. Pray for peace, and put your prayers into action. Each of us can do something to bring about peace.

WORK ON A PEACEMAKER CRAFT

Help children make a peacemaker craft to remind them to live in peace. Before gathering with the children, make copies of the words of Jesus: "Blessed are the peacemakers" (Matthew 5:9). Assemble craft supplies, including glue sticks, small foam hand stickers, and half sheets of colored card stock.

After talking with the children about what it means to be peacemakers, let them work on their peacemaker craft. Ask children to glue the words of Jesus to their card stock. Show them how to make a border with the hand stickers.

Let them work in small groups so they can help one another. This also helps shy children learn from what other children are doing. Encourage children to display the peace craft at home. Remind them that Jesus calls us to live as peacemakers in our lives.

PRAY ALWAYS

Prayer starter » *Jesus, help me to be a peacemaker by....*

Prayer to be peacemakers » *Jesus, Savior of all people, we pray for peace in our world. Give us the courage to live as peacemakers and work for justice for all people. We pray for an end to war and violence, which hurt so many people. May we bring hope to the lives of other people in your name. Amen.*

Jesus asks us to forgive

EXPLORE THE MESSAGE

Jesus always forgives us and asks us to forgive others. We encounter the forgiveness of Jesus in our lives each day. Jesus teaches us what it means to forgive

Jesus tells his disciples, "Forgive, if you have anything against anyone; so that your Father in heaven may also forgive you your trespasses."

» MARK 11:25

Forgiveness is a challenge for all of us. We must work at forgiving other people. Jesus teaches us about forgiveness by his words and actions.

Explore forgiveness with children:

- Forgive others as God forgives us.
- We must forgive even those who will never be sorry.
- Grudges only hurt us and can lead to an unhappy life.
- We cannot change others, but we can change our own hearts.
- Pray to Jesus for help in forgiving others.

We are to follow the example of Jesus in forgiving people who have hurt us. In this way we live as his disciples.

TALK ABOUT SITUATIONS

Children need practice in learning to forgive others. Discuss each situation below and ask them to share ideas with the group.

- A kid in your class says something mean about you and everyone laughs. Do you act grouchy the rest of the day? Do you try to get even? Do you make fun of someone else? Why not?
- One of your friends did something that really hurt your feelings. Should you ignore him the next time he talks to you? Is it OK not to be his friend anymore? How can you forgive and get past this?
- Your mom or dad yells at you for something you didn't even do. Do you yell back? Do you go out and slam the door? Is it OK to hold a grudge for days? Does prayer help? What else could you do?
- Someone in your family was hurt by the actions of someone else. Does forgiving them mean what the person did was OK? Is it good to talk to someone you trust about this? How do grudges hurt us?

This activity involves the children in thinking about real answers to situations. In this way they see that they must make choices in their lives. Stress that we cannot control what happens to us, but we can control how we react.

PRAY ALWAYS

Prayer starter » *Jesus, forgive me for the times I...*

Let go of grudges prayer » *Jesus, light of our lives, thank you for forgiving us for the things we have done wrong and for right things we have failed to do. Show us how to let go of grudges and anger so we can live as you show us. May we forgive others in your name. Amen.*

Jesus teaches us to forgive

EXPLORE THE MESSAGE

Jesus teaches his disciples that we are to be people of forgiveness in our hearts and in our lives. Walking with Jesus means walking in peace and forgiveness. Jesus is loving and merciful and always forgives us. Jesus wants us to share that mercy with others. Jesus stresses mercy and forgiveness in the gospels.

Jesus says to his disciples, "And if the same person sins against you seven times a day...you must forgive."

» LUKE 17:4

We cannot put a limit on how many times we will forgive others. It also doesn't matter if the person is sorry for what they've done. We are still to forgive them. This is to be a way of life for us as followers of Jesus. Jesus will help us do this. It takes a lot of prayer to forgive someone. In forgiving others we encounter the forgiveness of Jesus Christ in our lives.

Jesus teaches us to forgive other people. He forgave people, even from the cross! By our words and actions we witness to Jesus' love for all people.

DO AN ACTION PRAYER

Engage young children in praying to Jesus with an action prayer. Say the words and do the actions line by line. Then children repeat the words and actions.

Jesus action prayer:

Lord Jesus,	*point to palms*
we give praise to you	*arms overhead*
for all that you have done for us.	*hands over heart*
Help us to live as you did	*nod head yes*
and walk as your disciples.	*walk in place*
Give us the strength	*flex muscles*
to forgive other people	*arms outstretched*
as you forgive us.	*fist on heart*
May we follow your example	*walk in place*
and witness to your love	*cross wrists over chest*
for all people everywhere	*outstretched arms*
Amen.	*fold hands*

PRAY ALWAYS

Prayer starter » *Jesus, help me to forgive when...*

Forgiveness prayer » *Jesus, Lord of mercy, give us the strength and the courage to do what is right. Show us how to live the gospels and follow your example. Help us forgive those who have hurt us. May we be people of mercy and forgiveness each day. Amen.*

Jesus brings us new life

EXPLORE THE MESSAGE

Jesus brings us a message of hope. God loves us and is with us always. We are never alone. Jesus came for all people, past, present, and future. Jesus came for each one of us! We live in the light because of Jesus.

Jesus said to Martha,
"I am the resurrection and the life."

» JOHN 11:25

We can trust in Jesus, who wants only the best for us. Jesus teaches us that each person is important. Each person has a special purpose in life. Each of us has talents and gifts to share with others.

When the world seems to focus on negative things, it has an impact on children. War, violence, grudges, gangs, and people hurting other people all make children sad and afraid. Show them that we can have hope in Jesus and in the future.

Share with children that Jesus is always with us. Jesus brings new life to each of us! When life seems a challenge, we can turn to Jesus in prayer. We encounter Jesus when we live in hope. Encourage children to be hope-filled people who see the good in others and in our world.

SHARE HOPE WITH OTHERS

Jesus brings all of us new life. Alleluia! Encourage children to share hope in Jesus with others. As disciples of Jesus we can do this in big ways and little ways. We can bring hope to the lives of others by our words and actions.

Ways to share hope:

- Encourage someone who seems sad.
- Help another child learn something new.
- Introduce yourself to a new student.
- Share a skill, such as playing music.
- Donate personal care items to a shelter.
- Offer a smile to someone who is struggling.
- Say hello to an elderly person as they leave Mass.

PRAY ALWAYS

Prayer starter » *Jesus, I praise you for...*

Prayer of hope » *Jesus, thank you for the new life that you bring to all people. We rejoice in you and all that you have done for us. We thank you for the people who care about us and the people who teach us about you. Show us how to live as people of hope and to share hope in you with others. Amen.*

CHAPTER 7

Encounter Jesus in sharing the good news

Jesus teaches us about God's unending love for each of us. Through his life, death, and resurrection, Jesus brings new life to people of all generations. Jesus Christ calls us to carry on his mission to the world and all people. We encounter Jesus when we share the good news with others.

All people are invited to come and see who Jesus is. We can tell others about Jesus. We bring the good news of Jesus to our families, our schools, our neighbors, and our communities by what we say and do.

We are a church for everyone. Hopefully, the children of today will live this idea and share it with the next generation. We want them to know that Jesus came for all people and calls us to share the good news of new life for all people. Our walk with Jesus means walking with others.

We share our faith with the children, and we pass on to them the call to be missionary disciples in our world. Each of us is called to carry on the mission of Jesus Christ to our world so that all people will hear the good news.

Jesus walks with us

EXPLORE THE MESSAGE

After Jesus' resurrection, two disciples were walking to the town of Emmaus. A person came and joined them. The person was Jesus, but they did not recognize him. On the journey they listened to the man as he explained Scripture to them. Then at dinner, they finally realized who Jesus was in the breaking of the bread.

Jesus took bread, blessed, and broke it, and gave it to them. Then their eyes were opened and they recognized him.

» LUKE 24:30–31

As a result of their encounter with Jesus, the disciples return to Jerusalem to share the good news of Jesus Christ with other people.

Share the story of the journey to Emmaus with the children in your group (Luke 24:13–35). Explore with the children that we are to follow the example of the two disciples in telling others about Jesus.

We walk our journey to Emmaus:

- We open our hearts to encounter Jesus in our lives.
- We encounter Jesus in Scripture and the Eucharist at Mass.
- We have hearts filled with joy because Jesus is with us.
- We celebrate that Jesus came for each of us.
- We are called to share the good news with others.

We are called to tell other people ways that we have encountered Jesus in our lives. This helps them learn about Jesus. The endless love Jesus has for us is truly amazing!

CREATE A GROUP BUTTERFLY CROSS

Jesus brings us new life through his cross and resurrection. To help children remember that Jesus came for all of us, ask them to make a group cross for the area where you gather.

Cut a cross about sixteen inches high by twelve inches wide out of green poster board. Then give each child a large butterfly sticker to add to the cross. This is a visual sign of the resurrection and the new life that Jesus Christ brings to each of us.

Explore the idea that the risen Christ is with us always. We can walk in love by living as Jesus lived. We are called to share the good news of Jesus' resurrection with others in our lives, as the disciples did in theirs.

PRAY ALWAYS

Prayer starter » *Jesus, I know you are with me in...*

Prayer to encounter Jesus » *Lord Jesus Christ, we know that you walk with us as you walked with the disciples to Emmaus. Help us to see you at work in our hearts and our lives. We thank you for the new life you bring to all of us. May we encounter you in the words of Scripture and in the gift of the Eucharist at Mass. Show us how to live as people of the resurrection. Amen.*

Jesus brings us hope

EXPLORE THE MESSAGE

Jesus sends us to share with others all that he teaches. Jesus came for all people. The Holy Spirit helps us witness to Jesus Christ in our lives.

The risen Christ tells his disciples, "Go therefore and make disciples of all nations."

» MATTHEW 28:19

Our relationship with Jesus involves other people. As disciples we can help people encounter Jesus in their lives. Jesus brings us hope, and we can bring hope to the lives of other people. As a church and as individuals, we are to point the way to Christ for others. We share with others the joy and hope we have in being disciples of Jesus.

Share the good news:

- Jesus loves us with an unending love.
- Jesus came for all people.
- Jesus calls each of us to be his disciple.
- Jesus brings us hope now and forever.
- Jesus is with us always.

Each of us is called to share the good news of Jesus Christ with others. In this way other people learn that Jesus came for all of us. As we walk our journey with Jesus, we invite others to walk this journey too.

REFLECT ON A DISCIPLE MEDITATION

We can help children imagine that they are with the risen Christ when he teaches his disciples. Ask them to close their eyes or lay their head on their arms as you read the meditation based on Matthew 28:16–19.

> You are walking with the disciples of Jesus on the road to Galilee. As you go along, you talk about all that has happened. It has been a difficult time since Jesus died on a cross. It seems as if all hope is gone. Then the women came and said that Jesus had risen. Is Jesus really alive? How is this possible? You dare to hope that this is true.
>
> You keep walking. Suddenly you see a figure in the distance. As he gets closer you see that it is Jesus. Your heart is filled with joy at this amazing sight. You know now that everything Jesus taught is true. Your heart is filled with hope.

Then Jesus tells his disciples to go and make disciples of all nations. He says that he will be with us always. You know that Jesus is speaking to you too. You will answer his call. You can't wait to tell everyone this amazing news. Now open your eyes and come back to the group.

PRAY ALWAYS

Prayer starter » *Jesus, may I witness to the good news by...*

Make disciples prayer » *Jesus, Lord and Redeemer, you tell us to go and make disciples of all nations. May we share the good news with others in our families, our communities, and our world. Help us to bring hope to the lives of others. May we invite others to join our walk with you. Amen.*

Jesus calls us to share the good news

EXPLORE THE MESSAGE

Before Jesus ascends to heaven, he reaches out to his disciples. He tells them to carry on his mission to the world. This message is for disciples of all times and places.

Jesus appeared to his disciples and told them, "Go into all the world and proclaim the good news to all creation."

» MARK 16:15

When we encounter Jesus in our lives, we want to share the good news with others. It is too amazing to keep to ourselves. Jesus brings new life to all people. We are called to tell others what Jesus said and did. In this way, they encounter Jesus in their lives. We bring hope to the lives of other people in the name of Jesus Christ our Lord.

MAKE A DISCIPLE CROSS

Children learn best by seeing and doing. Help them learn about being disciples of Jesus with a group disciple cross. Before gathering with the children, cut a large cross from colored poster board. Put a sign in the middle that says: "Live as disciples of Jesus."

Then print words about being disciples. Print them by hand on colorful sticky notes. Include words such as the following.

- hope
- share
- love
- forgive
- care
- joy
- serve
- peace
- pray
- faith
- compassion
- trust

When you gather with the children, remind them that Jesus teaches us how to follow him by all he said and did. Talk with the children about ways we can live as his disciples.

To make the idea of being a disciple more visual, show them the cross and the message. Invite each child to take a sticky note. Then each child says the word out loud and puts it on the cross. Be sure you have enough so each child gets a turn.

Display the disciple cross with the sticky notes where your learners will see it. The cross will remind them of what it means to live as a disciple of Jesus Christ in our lives. As we walk with Jesus, we walk his way of love and hope for all people.

PRAY ALWAYS

Prayer starter » *Jesus, guide me to share hope with others by...*

Proclaim the good news prayer » *Lord of all people, you told your disciples to proclaim the good news of your life, death, and resurrection to all creation. Show us how to share our faith so others will come to know your love for all people. May we walk as your disciples each day. Amen.*

Jesus helps us live in joy

EXPLORE THE MESSAGE

It is so important for children to understand that there is joy and hope in being disciples of Jesus. Jesus wants us to live in joy as we follow him each day.

Jesus said, "I have said these things to you so that my joy may be in you, and that your joy may be complete."

» JOHN 15:11

We have joy in our hearts because of Jesus. We can find joy in the beauty of God's creation, in the unending love of the risen Christ, in people who care about us, and in a day filled with blessings. Each day is an opportunity to find joy! Ask children to name things that bring them joy.

Find joy in many ways:

- Go outside on a beautiful day.
- Be grateful for our blessings.
- Help someone with a project.
- Laugh with your friends.
- Know Jesus loves you.
- Spend time with people who love you.

Help children understand that we were created by God to live in joy. Joy is an important gift to share with children. Explain to them that we are called to share joy in Jesus with others. Joy is contagious. Joy helps us see the many blessings and gifts God has given us. We are called to rejoice in the love of Jesus for each of us.

SHARE THE JOY OF BEING A DISCIPLE

We must let people know that Jesus came for everyone. We can help other people encounter Jesus in their lives. It's important to remember that the cross has no meaning without the resurrection. Jesus brings joy to all of us through his life, death, and resurrection. Each day we are to walk as his disciples.

Ways to live as disciples of Jesus:

- Put Jesus first in your life.
- Share stories about Jesus with others.
- Show the love of Jesus by our actions.
- Find joy in serving others.
- Invite someone to Mass with you.
- Treat people of all races with respect.
- Bring hope and joy to the lives of others.

PRAY ALWAYS

Prayer starter » *Jesus, may I live in joy as your disciple by…*

Live in joy prayer » *Lord Jesus Christ, fill our hearts with joy in being your disciples. We thank you for the many blessings in our lives. Help us to follow you in all that we do. Guide our way so that we may welcome others. May we live in your joy each day and share that joy with others. Amen.*

Jesus sends us forth

EXPLORE THE MESSAGE

Jesus came for everyone. We carry on the work of Jesus to the world. On the first day of the week, the risen Christ came to where the disciples were gathered.

Jesus says to them,
"As the Father has sent me, so I send you."

» JOHN 20:21

This is our command too. We are called to share the good news of Jesus Christ with all people. In telling others about Jesus, we let them know ways we encounter Jesus in our own lives. We show who Jesus is by the way we live as his disciples. We joyfully witness to what Jesus said and did by our own words and actions. With the help of the Holy Spirit, we can carry the message of Jesus Christ to others.

The good news of Jesus' love for us can change people's lives. We can bring hope to others. The best way we can share the good news is by telling others what faith in Jesus Christ means in our lives. This personal touch helps people understand who Jesus is. We can tell others about the hope and joy that Jesus brings to each of us.

CREATE INDIVIDUAL CROSSES

Show children how to make colorful crosses to remember that we are sent to share the good news of Jesus Christ with others. Provide various colors of card stock and patterned washi tape. This paper tape comes in a variety of colors and patterns and is great for crafting.

Let children know they can each make a cross by first cutting out a cross from a half sheet of colorful card stock. Younger children may need the crosses precut. Each child decorates his or her cross with strips of washi tape placed diagonally across the cross. Be sure they leave room between the rows of tape. Show children how to trim off any extra tape all around the cross for a finished look.

Display the crosses if you have a bulletin board. The crosses look great on either side of a large cross representing Jesus. Or the children can take their crosses home to remember that Jesus Christ calls us to tell others the good news.

PRAY ALWAYS

Prayer starter » *Lord Jesus, help me tell others about you by...*

Message prayer » *Lord Jesus, Savior of all people, help us to carry on your mission to the world. We know that you call us to serve others as you did and proclaim the good news to all people. Send your Holy Spirit to help us share your message of hope with others now and always. Amen.*

ALSO BY PATRICIA MATHSON

33 Mass Lessons and Activities for Children

This practical book is a treasure trove of easy, meaningful, and enjoyable ways to introduce children to each part of the Mass and show them how the Mass connects with daily life. Activities for the classroom are supplemented with a family take-home page, with special recommendations for families with children preparing for First Eucharist. Ideal for religious education programs, Catholic schools, family faith formation programs, and more, this book will quickly become indispensable for busy catechists. *Pages are reproducible.*

72 PAGES | $16.95 | 8½" X 11" | 9781627853804

70 Church Year Lesson Starters for Kids

and those who teach them

From poster projects to prayer prompts, this engaging and meaningful collection of activities spans the church seasons from Advent and Christmas to Lent, the Triduum, Easter, and Ordinary Time. You'll find a variety of projects, ideas, and prompts to accommodate many learning styles, personalities, age groups, and settings. Organized by season, here are craft projects, service ideas, games, sharing questions, small group suggestions, prayers, ideas for exploring Scripture, and much more. Ideal for parish, school, or family settings.

96 PAGES | $9.95 | 5½" X 8½" | 9781627853057

ENRICHING FAITH

Prayers and Activities on Service

Help children make Christian service a way of life with this creative collection of outreach projects, hands-on learning experiences, and joyful prayers. Each activity speaks to children's hearts and includes easy instructions, curriculum connections, and more. Perfect for parish, school, or home-based programs, and anyone who wants to help children become caring and compassionate followers of Christ.

72 PAGES | $14.95 | 8½" X 11" | 9781585959372